Table of Contents

Welcome to Our Moment

What does our future have in store? Where is our country headed? And the favorite question of pollsters, are we going in the right direction? All these questions are leading to the much greater question of whether the America of the future will be as great as the America of the past. Once again we have reached another moment in our history when Americans must answer these questions and define our future. This election will be one of those elections that define a generation of Americans, where we as citizens must go to the ballot box and set the agenda for how we want to be governed, and what values America will uphold. We will with a loud voice give authorization to one of two opposing philosophies that will shape the America in which we will have to raise our children and guide them as they nurture our grandchildren.

Everyone should relish this moment. Very few times in one's lifetime will there be an election where it matters so much to be an American, because the rest of the world will be a stakeholder in America's future. With all the turmoil throughout the world, other nations are looking to America to lead the way and stand up for the values that we hold most precious. They will be watching and waiting to see what direction we choose.

Citizens around the globe, acting as observers, will take notice whether or not we embrace our mantra as a nation which cares for its diverse people, be they rich or poor, while providing opportunity for all those who venture to our shores.

There have been many elections in the past where Americans had to cast their vote on how and why wars were to be fought or how other citizens were to be recognized and treated. Americans of those generations were able to step up and reinforce the bedrock values which our forefathers used as the building blocks of our republic. Specifically, during the Civil War, we had to not only go to the ballot box to protect our ideals and guide our nation into the future; Americans had to spill the blood of our brothers in order to uphold the principles which made the United States great then, and continue to make America the greatest nation on the Earth. That generation of Americans was able with their might and their political will to lead America from a path of slavery to a time which saw black Americans achieve civil rights and equal status under the law. They were able to stop fellow Americans from holding on to misguided beliefs of the past and embrace the new wisdoms of the future. Fortunately, we do not have to spill the blood of our fellow Americans to put our future on a path to a greater tomorrow, but still we have to view this moment as our "Modern Civil War."

We are again at a pivotal hour in our history when our nation is completely divided on how we view our future. Not since the Civil War era, has our nation been so strongly polarized by the issues which confront us. It is somewhat ironic that the first black president stands before us as one of the choices to be re-elected president of the United States, because similar to the Civil War era, we have two diametrically opposed views of our future with one side absolutely unwilling to compromise on any solution that veers from the path they see for our nation. They believe that our future lies in reinstituting the dogmas of our recent past. The consequences of these misguided policies have caused us to suffer today from the beliefs of that past period. Additionally, this group wants to allow money and power to reside in the hands of a very few, while subjecting the rest of us to the merciless and blind free hand of market forces without sufficient regulations or interference. Furthermore, they want to take away the laws and programs, which were the result of generations of Americans exercising their right to put a stamp on America's future. Many fought and died for these programs over the last 150 years. Quietly but consistently, this group is pushing

4

to remove the social safety nets which were put in place by generations of the past when we desperately witnessed just how ruthless the free hand of the market can be during the Great Depression. Also, they want to reverse the civil rights acts and voting acts which allowed our country to take major steps closer to a *"more perfect union"*. Finally, they want to tell us how to live, whom we should love and the way we should define our families, and then tell us when we are in trouble that we are to blame because we are not taking care of our individual needs and responsibilities.

The other group, although flawed in its own ways, believes in the expansion of the middle class. This group sees the government as responsible for helping all people have the opportunity to reach the American dream. People of this group preach inclusion and the participation of all citizens and noncitizens, giving chances to those who may not have arrived at our shores in a legal manner. They scream for equal rights for all regardless of race, creed or sexual orientation. There is recognition that the world is a changing place and we must change our policies but never compromise our core values of, "We the people ...." Finally, this group, if it can embrace the fiscal responsibility to the next generation, strongly advocates that the problems we face today are solvable through the sacrifice of those who have the means, but the benefits will be reaped by all.

We must all engage and prepare to fight with our vote in this "Modern Civil War." No one who truly believes in the principles that are outlined in our Constitution can sit idly by on the sidelines and allow this election to be just like any other election in their lifetime. There is definitely too much at stake for all of us, as individuals and as a nation. We must all stand up and embrace our moment to make a difference.

With that being said I am embracing my moment through this book and the accompanying blog. I am in no way naïve enough to believe that this election will be a referendum on the policies of the other party; this election will be an assessment of the policies and vision of President Obama. It is due to this very reason that I have written this book outlining from my perspective why I believe President Obama must be re-elected and given an opportunity to guide us into the future. In the pages to follow I will describe in some detail how I have arrived at my conclusion. I will discuss President Obama as a person, look at his domestic policies and achievements, his foreign policies and achievements, and finally I will provide my opinion on the policies of the other party in more detail.

I know many of you must be asking, why my opinion should matter to anyone. I am not just trying to be arrogant; I truly believe that if someone sees my perspective on these issues it will at least give them a moment of hesitation and make them think about their own positions. At the very least, I hope that this book will help frame their arguments on the multitude of issues which face our nation. I discuss these issues from the point of view of an average American with the limited amount of information which we all have. I do not have any more information than anyone else, no special access, but that is how most of us will have to make this extremely important decision. We will have to wade through the many different news programs to find information which will help us formulate our opinions, or we will use our life experiences or the experiences of our friends and family to develop our basis of thought. I just wanted to give everyone an additional opinion, which, though maybe unsolicited, is only an attempt to make you as informed as possible. I welcome the opinions of opposing views as well as like-minded people on my blog at www.obamaforsecondterm.com. This kind of open dialogue is what will make our union stronger going into the future.

The Leader

Right Man for the Right Moment

As I become engrossed in the Olympic coverage, I am bubbling with pride as I watch the United States Olympians battle and compete in event after event for their dream of a gold medal. I envy the greatness of each athlete, and marvel at their determination and perseverance as they strive to overcome their own struggles and fears and defeat their opponents. Although each Olympian shares this incredible indelible spirit to succeed, I am most struck by the diversity of all our athletes. These Olympians come from all walks of life and from all ethnic and cultural backgrounds. It is obvious that the strength of Team USA lies in this diversity of athletes competing in a variety of events. The success of the overall team, as well as the success of each individual athlete, is a result of embracing this diversity. Each athlete draws strength from our "melting pot." So, as I look at the faces of all these athletes, I relish the fact that they are a colorful blend of all the people of America.

Furthermore, this diversity of our people, each having an enduring spirit, has always been the foundation of our nation. Many would have us believe that this nation is only great because of our white European origins and it is only these beginnings which were meaningful throughout our history. They discount the contributions of all those who slaved, battled and overcame oppression in order to make America a *"more perfect union."* However, it is truly these very struggles that have been the building blocks of our nation. President Obama embodies and is a product of these glorious victories resulting from these momentous battles of the past. He represents both the America of the past and the America of the future. There are those who are battling against the inevitable tides of the future; those who are trying to somehow hold on to the America of the past, where the face of America was a "white Anglo-Saxon Protestant" male. They believe that it is only through holding on to this misguided antiquated belief that America can be great going into the future. This is why we constantly hear statements declaring that, "we must recapture America", and we hear coded statements about President Obama that "he is foreign" or "does not understand America". They want us to believe that no person of color or of a different cultural background can truly be American. Consequently, President Obama cannot really be born in their America.

Our 530 Olympic athletes are but a microcosm of why this belief is so false. They illustrate that it is the diversity of our people which makes America the greatest nation on Earth and an envy of the rest of the world. No one better represents this diversity than President Obama. He is the epitome of the greatness which is America; a man who rose from humble beginnings to aspire to the highest office in the land. Only in America, as a result of the struggles of our people and the foresight of our founders, can someone strive and by means of achievement and opportunity navigate a path of such brilliance.

President Obama from the very beginning was able to combine his English and Kenyan heritages in order to foster that enduring spirit which is unique to America; where he is able to see America as the "land of opportunity." This perspective of America has driven immigrant groups throughout the world to our shores looking for a better life. It is this spirit which propelled President Obama to reach for the highest stars, and with his families' guidance he had all the tools to attain those lofty goals. He went to the best university in the land but aspired not to do what others had done and use his education for personal monetary gain, but utilize that education for the betterment of the nation he loved so much. He embraced his mother's pursuits by becoming a community activist and a professor of law. Finally, he entered the government as a local representative, then a senator and lastly as president in order to change the lives of many, not just a few. This path does not make him special; it makes him American, because only in America could such a life be possible.

Above all else President Obama embodies the values which keeps America strong and makes America great. He is a devoted husband and loving father, holding in the highest regard all the family values which so many advocate so loudly. In a time when role-model fathers are desperately needed, President Obama stands in the forefront by example illustrating openly that he relishes his responsibility as a father and enjoys every moment he is able to spend with his daughters. He demonstrates that even the most powerful man in the world can find time to coach his daughter's basketball team.

At last, probably the most important symbol, President Obama can illustrate for us is that as America transitions into a more colorful nation, our future greatness is possible even though we do not have a typical face from the past leading our way. America's future is dependent on leadership which will be very different from those who came before. We will have to embrace our diversity, truly believe in our melting pot in order to overcome the obstacles that lie in our future.

Metrosexual, Black Abe Lincoln

When I heard this description of President Obama by the authors of the "Defeat Barack Hussein Obama" proposal, I was intrigued by the comparison. I congratulate them for picking an analogous situation that is so apt for our time. I have always felt that President Obama had Lincolnesque qualities beyond the obvious similarities of being a young senator from Illinois that ascended to the Office of President. Each also shared the physical presence which exhibits a formidable sense of strength and an incredible stoic sense of character. All of their qualities were best demonstrated in the speeches they gave before captivated audiences, both while they were campaigning for the presidency and when they were in office. Each president had a case to prove to America that their vision of the future was a picture where everyone in America could prosper and achieve the dreams of our forefathers while adhering to the values which made our nation great.

President Lincoln, although officially a member of the Republican Party, would not be considered a viable candidate to be the presidential nominee of today's Republican Party. They would consider him far too liberal for their modern platform. He would never be considered a "true conservative." Many of

Lincoln's political beliefs with respect to education, labor rights, government spending, and overall role of the federal government are comparable to those championed by President Obama. The surprising policy similarities are obvious when one compares their speeches, but the parallel in their vision for their America is where each president's likeness is most apparent.

Each president in his Inaugural Address outlined his vision for one united nation. The most important component of that view they shared was their faith in the people of America to determine their own destiny and control their own future. Both presidents echoed the sentiments that the future of the country lay not in the institutions of the government but in the hands of the people. We have the power to change the institutions and amend the constitution which governs us. It is how we act toward each other and what we want America to be that will determine our future.

President Lincoln outlined in his speech that those who sent him to the White House did not want the spread of slavery outside the southern states, but that was for the people to say with a loud voice, as they as citizens exercised their right to control the future of the Union. He also recognized the rights of those who believed that slavery should continue and acknowledged their right to hold their opinions:

> One section of our country believes slavery is right, and ought to be extended, while the other believes it is wrong, and ought to not be extended. This is the only substantial dispute....This country, with its institutions, belongs to the people who inhabit it. Whenever they shall grow weary of the existing government, they can exercise their constitutional right of amending it, or their revolutionary right to dismember or overthrow it...I fully recognize the rightful authority of the people over the whole subject....

Similarly, the citizens who sent President Obama to Washington wanted him to shape a future where everyone of all diverse backgrounds would have a fair chance at the "American Dream." Additionally, they wished for an America where their children would have a chance to reach the heights which generations before were able to attain.

> For we know that our patchwork heritage is a strength, not a weakness. We are a nation of Christians and Muslims, Jews and Hindus - and non-believers. We are shaped by every language and culture, drawn from every end of this Earth; and because we have tasted the bitter swill of civil war and segregation, and emerged from that dark chapter stronger and more united, we cannot help but believe that the old hatreds shall someday pass; that the lines of tribe shall soon dissolve; that as the world grows smaller, our common humanity shall reveal itself; and that America must play its role in ushering in a new era of peace... For as much as government can do and must do, it is ultimately the faith and determination of the American people upon which this nation relies. It is the kindness to take in a stranger when the levees break, the selflessness of workers who would rather cut their hours than see a friend lose their job which sees us through our darkest hours. It is the firefighter's courage to storm a stairway filled with smoke, but also a parent's willingness to nurture a child, that finally decides our fate.

As President Obama may be the *Metrosexual, Black Abe Lincoln,* for certain, he does draw on the wisdom of our 16th President that we the people are what make this nation the greatest nation on Earth, and we must stand up united to meet the challenges which confront us. President Lincoln was faced with the daunting issue of slavery which eventually drove our nation to war. But President Lincoln was able to rely upon the strength and convictions of the people to guide his way to a brighter future. President Obama faces the wedge issue of fairness and how we are going to share the sacrifices which will be required in our future. Will President Obama have the strength and convictions of each of us to guide his way into the future?

A Card Carrying Member ...

The United States of America is the most unique and greatest country in the history of mankind because it is built completely on a set of shared values that reward individualism while preaching love for the community. President Obama is the result of this synergy. His personal story of achievement and success coupled with an unrelenting call to work for the betterment of his community as an activist, state representative, senator and president illustrates his passion to build a better America. He, like every president before him, wants to bring us closer to a *more perfect union*. As president, he took the oath of office to protect the Constitution and uphold the values which we covet so deeply, but in that oath he also accepted the obligation to defend the Constitution and the rights and protections it bestows on the citizens of the United States. To this end, President Obama's administration has explicitly defended gun rights in Washington, D.C., the borders in southwestern United States, voting rights of minorities all over America, the rights of Muslims to worship freely anywhere they choose, the right of a woman to choose, the rights of women to receive the same pay for the same job, the rights of gay soldiers to serve openly in the military, and most recently, the rights of gay and lesbian couples to marry and enjoy the same recognition as heterosexual couples.

The Republicans speak of individual rights but want to take away the rights of persons they deem as not meeting their standards of conduct or those who simply do not agree with their philosophy. This blatant hypocrisy is the underpinning of the Republican agenda. This agenda, although it outlines a set of policies which seem to promote individual responsibility and rights, does not defend the rights of women, gays and lesbians, African Americans and Latinos or any other minority group. These policies clearly just attempt to hold on to the status quo of the white male European majority. It is only through the maintenance of this heritage do they believe that America can sustain its greatness. This singular idea is why their agenda and their vision for the future are wrong for America.

America is much more than a single heritage or a single origin. It is the result of a clear-cut idea that our individual beliefs and differences do not subtract from our ability to form a union, but actually enhance our *more perfect union*. President Obama believes and defends this simple idea. He has embraced the expansion and inclusion of everyone who wants to be American, while the Republicans through different voting rights legislation throughout the country, for example, is trying to limit the ability of Americans to vote for their leaders or even have a say in our future. These initiatives are not strengthening our union; they are alienating many Americans. Is this how we protect the individual rights of our citizens, by creating laws, which under the cloak of protecting voters' integrity, are actually taking away or reducing the opportunity for voters to cast their ballots?

Does their end justify their means? Or, simply, does any end justify any means when it comes to individual rights? The Republicans, supposedly the party of individual rights, would answer a resounding *NO*. However, it is President Obama and his Justice Department which has to challenge these laws in state after state in order to maintain access for all Americans. For instance, in Ohio the Republican Secretary of State is limiting the hours of pre-election voting in order to restrict the ability of young and minority voters to make the time to cast their ballots. These measures of expanded pre-election hours were instituted in previous elections because they wanted to encourage these disenfranchised voters to cast their ballots. Now since these voters are not casting their ballot to Republican satisfaction, their rights are to be eliminated in order to guarantee a victory.

Is this the America of our founding fathers, where we limit our most basic individual rights as citizens in order to further an agenda? Would our founding fathers believe any agenda worth such a price? Republicans proclaim themselves as the most patriotic party, meaning they represent the principles by which America is founded; however, if they do not defend our most basic core values, how can we seriously embrace the remainder of their vision?

Commander in Chief

The title Commander in Chief brings with it an incredible sense of responsibility and duty. When our founding fathers placed this mantle upon the Office of President they built in this authority in order to ensure civilian control of the military. Also, by having a political leader of the military which was outside the military hierarchy our founding fathers sought to promote the will and desires of the citizens of the United States. This is additionally why they attempted to limit this power by requiring appropriation actions and oversight by Congress at required times because they did not want any commander in chief to assume dictatorial power over these forces. Therefore, in order to hold this title a president does not need previous military experience. He has the military leaders as an advisory panel, keeping him fully aware of the limitations and strategies of military action.

Every commander in chief throughout our history must consider with utmost thoughtfulness the well-being of our soldiers before placing them in "arms way". These troops are the sons and daughters of each American and their lives must be held in the highest regard, as one would hold the life of their own child. Their sacrifice for their country must never be done without forethought for the lives we are about to lose. This is the most important duty of the commander in chief.

As such, our standard of engagement for deploying our troops in any military conflict is that every occurrence must be well thought out, with a purpose that is squarely in our national interest and a specific military goal which would outline an exit strategy that will explicitly define the moment when our national interest is fulfilled and our troops can be victoriously withdrawn from battle. Our last two wars have not met this standard. Both the wars in Iraq and Afghanistan have failed to some degree to satisfy either of these requirements. Namely, never before has any president ordered American soldiers into a war of our own creation, as in Iraq. Every conflict in our history has been a reaction to the actions of a hostile force, either to defend ourselves or to defend other countries that were in our national interest. Iraq represents the only time in our history when a commander in chief deployed our military without defining our national purpose or outlining the goals of the mission. The Bush administration hid behind the cloak that they were searching for WMDs (weapons of mass destruction), however, many countries throughout our history have had or sought WMDs and had vicious dictators but the President and his advisers realized that placing our troops in such a vulnerable position based on imperfect intelligence was not worth the sacrifice. President Bush's "hawkish" stance on military intervention completely disregarded the health and well-being of our soldiers.

Furthermore, the war in Afghanistan, although having a purpose which was in our national interest, failed to meet the criteria of setting a military goal which would indicate when our troops could be withdrawn from combat. Some would argue that the moment when troops could leave Afghanistan is when there is a stable government; however, placing our military in the role of nation builders is completely outside the scope of their capacity. It took political leaders to build our nation after the American Revolution. Thus, it is only through strong political leadership as our founding fathers exhibited during our inception that Afghanistan will find a stable future. Put simply, a military force cannot build a nation, and it is not the responsibility of our military to orchestrate such a project. So this as a goal is not a realistic military goal.

Consequently, President Bush failed to fulfill his most important duty as commander in chief, looking out for the welfare of his soldiers. The Republican presidential candidate is advocating the same "hawkish" positions with respect to the many conflicts and hotspots all over the globe. Mitt Romney wants to threaten attacking Iran and revive the Cold War of the 1970s with Russia. Additionally, he speaks of putting our troops in Syria but does not tell us if he would remove the troops from Afghanistan. Another Bush-type commander in chief would be detrimental to the well-being of our sons and daughters in uniform. How many more lives are we willing to sacrifice, without having an adherence to our standard of engagement?

President Obama has truly performed admirably in the role of commander in chief. He has adhered to our standard of engagement and has begun the process of cleaning up the Bush wars. He has ended the war in Iraq, has established a withdrawal date for the war in Afghanistan, and with the death of Usama Bin Ladin he has achieved the original military goal of the mission. In conjunction with these on-the-battlefield accomplishments, the Obama administration has made it a priority to care for wounded soldiers and their families. President Obama by strongly supporting legislation which fully funds our veteran services, such as VA hospitals and rehabilitation center, is establishing programs to treat PTSD (post-traumatic stress disorder) and other mental illnesses resulting from combat. His administration has further initiated a modern GI bill which tries to help veterans acclimate to civilian life, through providing new educational opportunities. President Obama has, most importantly, honored with dignity those who have fallen in the line of duty, and given their families closure and reassurance that their sacrifice has not been in vain. This portrayal of the sacred role of the commander in chief is how our founders envisioned it when they wrote the Constitution.

Here At Home

On Day One

Seemingly, every candidate for the highest office in the land wants to describe in detail his mental picture of his first day as the most powerful leader in the world. Each elaborately illustrates his policy priorities with unwavering conviction. However, as President Obama realized as he readied himself to take the mantle of president, as a candidate you are only privy to a minute amount of factual details showing what is really happening in the country. It was only after winning the election, during his transition period that he truly found out how close the country was to the next great depression or how entrenched we were in the two wars we were fighting. Many candidates on the campaign trail including President Obama acted on the premise that the day they assumed the Office of President, their policies and agenda for the country would now be the prevailing governance, regardless of what the previous presidents had done.

Governor Romney in stump speech after stump speech outlines that he is going to repeal this and by executive order do this other thing and then direct Congress to pass some other bill. This aggressive agenda although impressive in its accomplishments for one day, is quite unrealistic in its possible actual outcome. It is quite naïve to believe that in our present government much can be accomplished in one day, especially the first. Consequently, what we are invariably voting on is the direction in which each candidate wants to take the country. Their actual policies, while necessary for understanding their vision for their presidency, is merely a wish list for the future, and like most wish list we usually never receive all that is listed.

President Obama when elected on November 4, 2008 brought to the office the hopes of millions of Americans. He energized the electorate like few presidents had before him. He was able to inspire many groups of citizens who had never before participated in the electoral process, and to foster a belief that they could see true change in the system. Although for many reasons some of President Obama's policy promises were not able to come to fruition, his vision and direction for the country has been steadfast throughout these previous four years.

President Obama's vision of hope and fairness for all citizens of the United States has truly been his constant bedrock value throughout his presidency. For example, he has repeatedly fought for unemployment benefits and payroll tax cuts for those who have been caught in the grips of this slow-growing economy, even having to compromise with Republican leaders in the Congress in order to ensure their continued funding. One of his policy promises was the elimination of the Bush tax cuts for the wealthiest Americans, but as a result of these compromises he has not been able to balance the tax code and demand a fair contribution from those Americans who had gained so much during the Bush years.

We all would like to further believe that as soon as we elect a new leader to take the baton of president, the policies of the previous administration no longer have any effect on our nation. But as in a relay race, when the baton is passed to the next leg of the relay, the receiving athlete is dependent on the position the previous person has left him in.   In the case of presidential succession, the legacy of previous administrations will be felt for years to come throughout the country. President Obama was unfortunately left with the policies of President Bush. These policies created a federal budget deficit of $1.4 trillion and a growing federal debt of near $10 trillion. He also inherited two unfinished wars which were costing the nation billions of dollars each week, a banking crisis, a collapsing auto industry, deflationary property values in the housing market and a plummeting stock market. However, the worst result of these traditional Republican policies was the unfulfilled promises of the Bush tax cuts and his deregulatory agenda to create and sustain job growth in the economy. Over the Bush years, job growth in the country actually declined. When President Obama took the oath of office on January 20, 2009 the economy was losing 750,000 jobs per month.

In contrast, when President Bush took the oath of office on January 20, 2001, he was given the baton with a federal budget surplus of $236 billion and as a consequence, a shrinking federal debt of under $5 trillion. This debt primarily was the result of the Reagan tax cuts of the early '80s. President Clinton and Speaker Gingrich together were able to reform the welfare system, which now rewarded those who sought to better their lives, not just give recipients an endless cycle of dependency. Additionally, President Clinton over his eight years in office created over 23 million new jobs, and an incredible growth in wealth due to the expansion of the Internet. Furthermore, there was a flourishing housing market which increased the wealth of the middle class, and gave everyone, who worked hard, a chance at the American dream. All of these positive developments in the country were done through bipartisan compromise from both sides of the aisle. The period was marked by the development of policies which encompassed the strengths of both parties.

President Obama has not had this bipartisan compromise. The Republican leadership stated unequivocally that their number one priority was to make him a one-term president. The Republican congressional leadership has even been unwilling to work with President Obama on policy issues which have traditionally been championed by Republican lawmakers. Over the last four years, the Republicans have had more filibusters in the Senate than any other time in history, and after the midterm elections the Republican-controlled House of Representatives has consistently tried to dismantle the policies of the previous Congress, with 33 attempts to repeal the president's signature health care act, and making no attempt to find common ground on any of President Obama's policy objectives.

This unwillingness to help President Obama govern the nation has seemingly created a void in governmental leadership, causing the electorate to have a loss of confidence in the government as a whole. Our historically divided partisan government begs the question of why such a resolute division. Only during the Civil War has our nation been so divided among such distinct philosophical lines. The political discourse has even risen to the level of obstruction and disrespect for President Obama and more importantly the Office of the President. It has been suggested that it is because President Obama is African-American that the discourse has reached such a negative and disruptive level, but I only hope that this simplistic explanation is not the case. However, without cooperation and basic mutual respect for the views of opposing lawmakers our ability to resolve the many daunting problems which confront our nation will be greatly handicapped, regardless of which party occupies the White House. Hence, if Governor Romney wishes to accomplish all of his lofty first-day objectives, he will need to get much more cooperation than President Obama received on his day one.

Majority Rule

"Give me your tired, your poor,
Your huddled masses yearning to breathe free,
The wretched refuse of your teeming shore.
Send these, the homeless, tempest-tossed to me,
I lift my lamp beside the golden door!"

-Emma Lazarth

Oh, how times have changed! America is no longer the place where these words ring true. Our present debate on immigration completely forgets about our country's history, when we were the destination for all those who wanted to improve their lives. We welcomed those who landed on our shores looking to make a better life for themselves and their children. Ellis Island was established as the entry point for millions of Americans, who would be considered illegal immigrants today, because they did not, as Governor Romney said, "wait for their turn in line in their native country...", so that they could be processed and put on their path to becoming an American.

These immigrants which migrated to America by huddling on overcrowded boats during the late 19th and the early 20th centuries came with the same look in their eyes and the same zest for a better life, as the illegal immigrants who come to America today by air and stay too long, or by running across a river and jumping over or crawling under fences. We immediately presented those early immigrants with a means for them to obtain legal status; is that not what the processing station at Ellis Island was? All we asked of those who entered the United States was if they were healthy or a criminal. Additionally, we demanded that they have the means to take care of themselves and those who they brought with them. We required this so that they and their families would not become a burden on the rest of us. In those days, all it took was for someone to have $20 or $30 in their pockets to indicate the ability to support oneself or have family members in America vouch for them, and their path to citizenship was outlined like the *"yellow brick road."*

Where did our open arms policy go? Do we no longer need these highly motivated immigrants? Or just the ones that wait in lines? Of course, those who wait in lines and migrate legally to America must and always will have priority in the immigration process. Additionally, the world in which we live presently dictates that we know who is entering and leaving our borders. However, we have always welcomed these "huddled masses" that bravely jumped in boats and came to our shores. These immigrants with an *"America or die"* attitude have always been the zesty, adventurous additions to our melting pot. It has been an American tradition to leave the torch lit for these weary fortune-seekers. These immigrants have brought with them new knowledge, new leadership, new innovation, new energy, new ideas and most importantly, a new positive determination which reinvigorates everyone in our society.

If we have now chosen to disregard our heritage, should we penalize those who came here under our old belief system? We failed to provide them with their Ellis Island. Consequently, we must, in order to be true to our values, provide those who are illegal now and their children a path to residency and eventually citizenship, as we have done for the many generations before.

President Obama proposed this very idea in the "Dream Act" which passed the Democratic House, but got filibustered in the Senate by the Republicans in 2009. If this is consistent with our history, why would the Republicans block it now? President Reagan passed his own version of the "Dream Act" in the mid-1980's, because he knew that it was our tradition to provide this path to all those who quested after this cherished dream.

So, again why do the Republicans block it now? Plain and simply the Republicans are trying to hold on to the fleeting majority rule of the paler melting pot. The only difference between the illegal immigrants of today and the ones of our early history is their place of origin and the shades of their skin. Thus, the true immigration debate is not about borders, which we all agree must be secured for national security, or about validity of immigrants; it is fundamentally about numbers. If we provide these 12 million presently illegal immigrants a path to citizenship it will speed up the inevitable process towards a white European minority, as a result giving the colorful minority population majority rule.

There are those who believe an America without a white European majority can never maintain its status as the greatest nation on Earth. Governor Romney is catering to this constituency, and this is why he cannot be seen as one who endorses the "Dream Act." However, what Governor Romney and this constituency are not considering is that it has always been America's diversity that has made her the greatest nation on Earth; never merely the efforts or values of any one group, but the collection of strengths from all the groups. It is the uniqueness of this mixture that has made America what it is today.

Fortunately, as long as we hold to the ideas and values which our founding fathers encompassed in our Constitution, it really does not matter which group holds majority rule. Because being an American is a state of mind and an attitude which is inherent in all who wish to live in this great nation. Also, it is the belief above all else in the concepts, that the founding fathers held most paramount, which will allow America through the adherence to these convictions to continue to be the place for *DREAMERS*.

Keep the Government Away From My Medicare

It is quite astonishing how an issue which is so vital to our lives as health care can have so many mistruths and misconceptions. Our health care and the care of our families is without exception the most important issue which we as Americans must consider, and the average American citizen knows very little about how it is administered or how it is best distributed throughout our society. We continually ponder over the question of whether the access to affordable health care is a right or a privilege. Our founding fathers were not able to foresee this complex dilemma, thus were unable to provide us guidance with respect to this issue. We have had to find our own path. Our previous generations when faced with this issue chose to provide a social safety net for those who were most vulnerable. As a result, Medicare was created in order to try to protect all of us who later in life would require the most assistance, but have the least means to obtain it.

It is now our turn to complete the process previous generations have started. Thus, the issue we truly face today is not over the Affordable Care Act per se, but over how we will treat each other with respect to health care. Simply put, are we able to stand by and watch fellow citizens not get treatment for their conditions, because they do not have health insurance? Just like most issues in this election we are confronted with two diametrically opposed philosophies on whether health care is a right of all citizens, and, if so, how should we best provide health care to everyone. We currently have mandatory care laws in place which require hospitals to care for patients regardless of their ability to pay. This seemingly has answered the initial question. We as a society have chosen to help those who come to a hospital and present their condition. However, the cost of this emergency care to our society in terms of additional premiums on health insurance policies and the increased cost to hospitals is astronomical. So without some sort of universal health coverage, this cost burden will cripple us all.

Consequently, the Affordable Care Act was created to solve these problems in our health care system and to hold each American responsible for their health care, by requiring through a penalty or tax that each person must purchase health insurance. Additionally, it is a compromise between those who favor private sector control of health care and those who want a single payer system, like the previous generation chose when they created Medicare and Medicaid. The Act is definitely not socialized medicine, which has been claimed by its critics. It requires the involvement of private insurance companies in a very common sense way. The reason for the mandatory participation part of the Act, which most liberals really do hate, was to appease insurance companies. This clause was included to increase the revenues of insurance companies as compensation for requiring them to cover people with pre-existing conditions. The Act also expands Medicaid to allow those who cannot afford health coverage to get coverage, which should result in an actual lowering of cost to the entire society because there would be no need for all the numerous uninsured emergency room visits. This portion of the Act is paid for by taxing high-end health care plans, and, as a result, continuing to share the burden throughout the entire society. Furthermore, the Act makes preventative care visits free, allows students to stay on their parent's policy until they are 26, and actually refunds a percentage of our insurance premiums that are not used on medical bills, limiting operational cost of insurance companies to 20% of premiums.

There definitely is not much in this Act which would signal to anyone that we are now a socialist country, as some try to state, and there are no outrageous provisions, such as death panels, which should scare anyone. I would recommend that any concerned citizen should go on the Internet and download for themselves a copy of the Act. This Act does attempt to share the responsibility of health care, something already done through mandatory care laws. So as I said before if the Affordable Care Act is not what the debate is about, what is the real debate?

Again, it just seems obvious that we are truly debating over whether we as a society should accept a policy of sitting idly by and allow those who do not have health insurance or cannot afford health insurance to not receive proper medical treatment. Specifically, there are those who believe health care is a privilege not a right, and even the mandatory care laws should be repealed. In the Republican primaries, an audience in one debate cheered the notion of allowing someone who could not afford health care to die because they did not take responsibility for their health coverage. Is this the country we want to be, the country our soldiers have fought and died to defend? Are these our values?

We have gone all around the world advocating for human rights and have tried to impose sanctions and embargoes on countries, even deploying our soldiers, in order to defend those basic rights. However, here at home, we are willing to allow people to prematurely die because we do not want to provide our citizens with access to medical care when it is readily available.

The Republicans have tried to repeal the Affordable Care Act 33 times, without offering a replacement plan which would cover the 30 million uninsured citizens, who the Act now covers. When asked by reporters what they plan to replace the Act with, they shrug off the question. Or they provide details on a voucher solution that every independent group has said will not cover those 30 million uninsured. Additionally, there are many Republican governors who refuse to implement the Medicaid expansion portion of the Act, which is 90% paid for by the federal government. They are choosing not to provide their citizens with coverage that will be available to other Americans.

Call the Affordable Care Act what you will, even *Obama Care,* if it pleases everyone. The Act is clearly a step forward in the process which was started by prior generations. It is undeniably, as affirmed by the Supreme Court, a landmark piece of legislation which took a long time to negotiate and structure, but is consistent with our values and brings us closer towards a *"more perfect union."*

Are Tax Cuts Always the Answer?

In the Republican presidential primary campaign of 1980, presidential candidate Governor Ronald Reagan introduced to the world his new economic theory called *supply-side economics*. The heart of his theory was that the federal government through fiscal policy could stimulate economic activity by implementing marginal rate tax cuts which would give suppliers and investors incentive to produce more goods and services. This stimulation to the supply side would theoretically create its own demand. Additionally, the losses in tax revenue as a consequence of the marginal rate cuts would be offset by the increase in overall revenue resulting from the expansion of economic activity. This theory was a departure from the Keynesian theory of using fiscal policy for demand stimulation which was used during the prior 50 years. Governor Reagan's primary opponent in the Republican primaries was George H.W. Bush, a lifetime politician and ex-Director of the CIA. After hearing the details of Governor Reagan's new theory, candidate Bush called the theory, "*voodoo economics.*"

Upon winning the election, President Reagan and his Budget Director David Stockman introduced these tax cuts to the nation in their first budget in 1981. At that time, the nation was experiencing a stagflationary recession, which describes a period of high interest rates coupled with a high rate of unemployment. President Reagan, the great communicator, with the majority of the nation behind him, was able to pressure and cajole the democratically controlled Congress to pass his experimental budget plan, promising that this budget would be the much needed remedy for the ailing economy. Over the next few years the effects of the tax cuts were arguable, but in every budget following, President Reagan ran government deficits that grew larger and larger in each consecutive budget. He increased defense spending to the highest level in American history in response to America's new position as the *"Lone Super Power."* By the election of 1984, the economy was starting to strongly rebound, and by 1986 the economy was growing at a robust rate. President Reagan and the other Republican leaders hailed supply-side economics as the miracle remedy that saved the American economy. Tax revenues because of the robust economy were higher than the pre-recession revenues. The only downside to the Reagan economy was the increasing federal budget deficits and the growing federal government debt, which usually resulted in a crowding out effect of investment due to high interest rates, but with monetary policy now focused on keeping interest rates low in order to fight inflation, interest rates were kept consistent.

Since the apparent success of these policies during the Reagan administration, most Republican candidates and lawmakers adopted Reagan's supply-side economics, or sometimes called "trickle down" economics, as the accepted economic principle in the Republican political platform. However, even though George H.W. Bush was the Vice President under President Reagan for the entire eight years of his administration, when Bush became president in 1988, after promising in the campaign not to raise taxes, dramatically stating, "Read my lips, no new taxes.," he raised taxes in order to eliminate the ever-increasing budget deficits, and also pay for the cost of the troop deployment needed to defend Kuwait. This increase in taxes according to most Republicans was the reason for President Bush's defeat in the 1992 elections. Most Republicans resented President Bush for going against the policies of President Reagan, and thought he deserved losing the election. However, it can be argued that it was these tax increases which allowed President Clinton to balance the federal budget and even create the largest budget surplus in history, while still having the largest economic expansion in American history.

In 2000 with the election of President George W Bush, Republicans were reenergized by this new Bush's campaign promise to reinstitute *"Reaganomics."* Although the nation was experiencing the longest economic expansion in American history coupled with a federal budget surplus, candidate George W Bush promised to keep the expansion flourishing with new supply-side economic policies. President Bush in 2001 submitted a budget that called for the dramatic marginal rate tax cuts. He and his administration, many of whom were holdovers from the Reagan years, vehemently advocated that these tax cuts would, as they seemingly had during the Reagan administration, produce jobs and stir economic growth while still increasing government revenues. President Bush with a Republican-controlled Congress instituted the entire Reagan economic playbook.

This time, however, it is dramatically clear that *Reaganomics* failed to produce any of its desired results, and definitely was not the answer to prolonging a period of economic growth. It simply made a robust economy, weak and unstable. By 2008, the promises of these policies never materialized. The only outcome that mirrored those of the Reagan years was the incredible federal budget deficits and the corresponding explosion of federal debt, which had been left behind by the previous tax cuts. There was no job growth, no sustained expansion of economic activity and no increase in government revenues.

Furthermore, the deregulation that was coupled with the Bush tax cuts caused our financial institutions to teeter on the brink of collapse.

In 2008, candidate Obama campaigned on the promise of ending the Bush tax cuts for the top 1% of wage earners in the nation; but because of compromises he had to make, while president, in order to maintain other legislative priorities, he has not been able to correct this faulty policy. As a result, we continue to suffer from the failings of this invalid economic theory. President Obama must only look at these policies to see why he cannot lower the unemployment rate or get any consistent robust growth in the economy, regardless of how much fiscal or monetary stimulus is pumped into the economy. These Bush tax cuts have siphoned all monies out of the hands of the middle class and accumulated these dollars in the pockets of the wealthiest Americans, a trend which is obviously unsustainable.

Again, President Obama in his re-election campaign is calling for the elimination of these tax cuts for the wealthiest Americans. Truly these tax cuts need to be eliminated for everyone. Under President Clinton we had vigorous economic growth without these cuts, but Obama's Republican opponent, Governor Romney, is calling for further marginal rate tax cuts in order to cure our economic ailments. Governor Romney's solution is to give the patient cancer in order to cure the flu. Can we survive another experimental treatment of *Reaganomics*?

Jobs, Jobs, Jobs

With unemployment currently above 8%, every pundit, expert and newsperson keeps saying this election is only about jobs, jobs, jobs. Each candidate responds to this rhetoric by trying to demonstrate they are the one who truly understands how to create jobs. Governor Romney has tried to build his entire campaign around this very notion. He has repeatedly told us due to his private sector experience he understands how to create jobs. The Romney-Ryan ticket, actually for that matter most Republicans, advocate that the government must "step out of the way" and allow the private sector to create jobs. They outline a program of reducing taxes on "the job creators," reducing government regulations, and cutting government spending, which will result in growth in the private sector, thus creating jobs. On the other hand, President Obama and the other Democrats believe government does have a role in job creation. They are in favor of stimulus programs and other government spending programs, "priming the pump," as they say, in order to promote growth in the private sector, which will result in job creation. Consequently, we are faced with a choice which goes well beyond just jobs. It is a fundamental philosophical question about how we see the role of government in the economy and society.

We as Americans with our inherent puritan background and our rebellious nature are preordained to believe governmental control or intervention has in most cases had negative effects on our lives. We subscribe to the dogma that the government is an outside entity, independent of its people. However, this notion is absolutely false. Our government, through the incredible foresight of our founding fathers is a true reflection of our collective thoughts. Each representative whom we elect to office reflects the desires and attitudes of the district and state which they represent. It is through the coming together of these representatives where we can find common ground on issues which are important to all Americans. In addition, if we collectively agree that something is wrong with our policies of government, we have the capacity to change and adjust our government as we deem necessary. Generations after generations before us have been able to make corrections to our government through debate, collaboration of ideas and eventual compromise which has led us closer to a "more perfect union." Only one time in our history have we failed to utilize the genius which is our Constitution in order to find a solution to the issues, causing a division in our union. In this case, we had to resort to war among ourselves in order to convince those who would not compromise their hardened beliefs. Other than this time, where we as a people failed ourselves, our government has stood tall against foreign invading forces; brought us out of depressions; built the amazing structures which provide us energy and fuel; constructed our massive railroad and highway systems; propelled us to the moon; and plugged us all into the Internet.

These accomplishments have been through our collective efforts, because we are our government. It is too easy for us to say, "the government did it," thus relinquishing ourselves of the responsibility which our founding fathers put in our hands. Therefore, it is equally too easy to say, "Government should just step out of the way." This *laissez faire* approach to the society, economy, and specifically, job creation has failed to accomplish its desired objectives almost every time we have tried it throughout our history. This approach is simply putting in the hands of a few Americans our collective destiny. The government, because it is the reflection of our collective will, is the only way the majority of us can have some control over our collective future.

For many black Americans it was only through the acts of government that we were able to have the right to vote; able to send our kids to better schools; able to drink and eat at any fountain or restaurant we wish; and able to have a somewhat equal opportunity at a job. For American women it is only through the acts of government that they are able to vote; able to have choice over their bodies; and under President Obama, able to get equal pay for equal work. For all minority groups, it is government which has given equal voice to all Americans. Even for the majority of Americans, it is government that has enabled us to have a 40-hour work week; enacted child labor laws; built better schools for our children; constructed safer highways for us to drive on; and tried to secure our future in old age. And I say it again: we are the government, so to diminish the role of government is to eliminate our collective control of our future.

Many would twist this argument into me advocating for governmental control of everything or even go so far as to say I am endorsing socialism or communism; this is definitely not the case. I truly believe in the private sector and the strength of a capitalist economy as the engine for growth of a society, but just like any engine it must be monitored, maintained and sometimes fine-tuned. The individual pieces of the private economy should not be and are not responsible for the economy as a whole; this responsibility lies in the hands of our collective self, our government.

What Debt Crisis?

Sound the alarm, we have a debt crisis. Government spending is out of control. We are going to leave our future generations insurmountable debt. These sentiments and many others are being echoed throughout the chambers of Congress and on the streets of cities and towns everywhere throughout the United States. However, the people who are yelling these arguments the loudest are the ones who, in the middle of our so-called "debt crisis," want to reduce the income which is being received by government, by slashing the tax rates on those most affluent in our society. Does it make sense when we cannot already pay our bills to give tax breaks to those who have previously gained so much from our deficit spending? Should they not now pay some of their gains back to the rest of us?

Plainly, does it make sense to reduce the income of our government when we have so many bills to pay? Those screaming at the top of their lungs that we are in a debt crisis would like us to believe unburdening the wealthiest among us will give them money to further invest and do more business, thus, eventually "trickling down" to us lowly souls at the bottom. Furthermore, this increased economic activity will subsequently provide more tax revenues to the government. Did that work so well when President Bush did it in 2001? Oh yes, it would have worked if 9/11 had not happened and we had not engaged in two wars. But can we foresee the next 9/11? Should we not be prepared with a healthy country rather than one that is dependent on an economic theory which is based on money "trickling" from the pockets of the few to the hands of the many?

If this is the theory they wish to use to solve our debt crisis and promote our economic well-being, is there really a crisis or are they just yelling loudly out of political convenience? Because not only did this theory not reduce debt under President George W Bush, it created massive debt under President Reagan when he used "trickle-down economics" in the 1980's. Remember it was Vice President Dick Cheney that said, "President Reagan proved that deficits don't matter..." So invariably if deficits do not matter debt must not either. Simplistically speaking, would any household in order to pay off their debts cut their income and hope that this reduction will in the future result in more economic activity, which hopefully will bring more income into the household, while they fall further into debt? In the meantime, the household cuts their spending on necessities, like food and health care, just so that the person making the most in the household could drive a Lamborghini. Is this really a solution?

If there is really a debt crisis, would it not be economically prudent to increase the amount of income received by the government by increasing the taxes on those who could afford it the most and not bet our fiscal future on a historically proven failed economic theory? This can be easily accomplished by just moving the tax levels back to where the budget had a surplus and the economy was healthy; is this action truly not our only rational course of policy? It would be as if we were rebooting a computer and going back to the last good start-up. Any other course would be totally speculative. We know the results of what happened under the Clinton administration.

There must not really be a debt crisis, because the resolution to the crisis is quite simple. Just like in every debt situation, someone's debt burden is dependent on their income. If I do not have enough income to pay my obligations, I must increase my income and lessen my obligations. But the most important part of the equation is increasing my income because what is a big debt to someone making $20,000 per year is not a big debt to someone making $1 million per year. Hence, to advocate so loudly about a debt crisis and take raising revenue off the table is merely nonsensical.

Consequently, the Republican overreaction to the debt situation must be for political expedience, so that the wealthy few can get another tax cut and we can eliminate some of those dreaded progressive programs, such as Medicare and Social Security. If this is the case, stand up and just say that we, the Republicans, believe the social safety net is unnecessary and everyone should fend for themselves. Do not hide behind a veil of debt crisis and falsely tell the American people they care about these programs. Tell us their true agenda and then let us decide if we believe in their policy objectives and their economic and fiscal theories. By hiding behind all these fabricated arguments, it seems they realize their policies will only help the few and hurt the many.

The Real Job Creators

Everywhere in the media, on Wall Street and on Main Street there has been much debate about which group in our economy is the driving force behind the creation of jobs. Simply, who are the "Job Creators" in the economy? The Republicans want us to believe that the wealthiest citizens in our society are the ones who create the jobs. They want us to accept as fact that because these individuals invest, run and own the businesses which hire employees, these wealthy Americans create the jobs which keep the economy operating. Thus, Republicans advocate that we must give these individuals tax incentives, in the form of tax cuts, in order to keep the rest of us working. Although this is a plausible sounding theory, in reality, no business investor, executive or owner wants to create a job except if the creation of that job makes him more profit or saves him money resulting in more profit, because maximizing profit is the only incentive in any business. Plainly, the creation of a job is not a businessman's first priority. To a businessman the creation of a job is an additional expense which reduces profit and no single tax incentive is going to be able to compensate him for this ongoing expense, so jobs are only created if there will be additional substantial profit well above the cost incurred by the new hire. Hence, jobs are created by these wealthiest Americans only out of the necessity to achieve higher profits.

The Democrats, on the other hand, learned from the past and look back to over 50 years ago when previous generation of Americans answered the question of who were the *real job creators* in the economy. This generation of Americans who were returning from the battlefields of Europe or from war-related industrial jobs following World War II recognized that they had to establish and build a new peacetime economy. This generation realized that the growth in this new domestic economy and eventually the restructured world economy would only be possible if we built a strong American middle class, a middle class which was unique in world history. This group would have the buying power to drive the economic activity in this new consumer-oriented economy. This new middle class would have to be able to afford the new products which were going to be coming to market. They would have to be able to afford the houses which would be built; they would have to be able to afford the new cars and televisions which would revolutionize the American society; and most importantly, they would have to be able to afford to send themselves and their children to colleges and universities, so that America could have the most productive and educated workforce for generations to come.

As a result, in order to achieve these lofty goals, this new middle class required higher incomes; it needed loan programs in order to finance their cars and their homes; and it required educational assistance in order to afford the many colleges and universities offering higher education. Therefore, the federal government passed laws to help citizens unionize so they could get higher wages and additional benefits. Also, the government with the assistance of the recovering banking system created loan programs to help people afford houses and cars, giving veterans special programs so they would be rewarded for their service to our country. Additionally, this generation through their representatives created student loan programs and the GI Bill in order to give those who wanted to improve their education and the education of their children the means to afford the college of their choice.

All these programs open the door to millions and millions of Americans giving them the ability to move into the new middle class. It permitted these Americans to purchase their own home, drive their own car, watch their own TV, and see themselves and their children graduate from some of the greatest institutions of higher education in the world. In addition, these programs enabled those few to not only have upward mobility into the middle class, but also into the wealthiest groups in the country. The notion of the "American Dream" was born, which meant that anyone who was willing to work hard and persevere would be able to achieve whatever success level he wished in America.

For America, as a whole, this new vibrant middle class sparked an economic boom. This boom unlike the previous booms of other generations was broad-based and included an element of sustainability because this new middle class was just starting to grow. This new workforce was highly motivated and equally highly educated enabling them to establish, invest and own new businesses. The entrepreneurial spirit was flourishing and would lead to incredible innovations for years to follow. This new middle class also was able to absorb the influx of new Americans into the country, who were here to seek their own opportunity to achieve the "American Dream."

Consequently, should we not today follow the road map of our previous generation? The generation we call the "greatest generation." The generation, which fought wars in the name of freedom, stood tall to make America a *more perfect union*." They tackled the big issues, such as equal rights here at home, and worked together to overcome oppression and dictatorships all across the globe. We are the product of this generation. However, will we undo all they accomplished or follow in their footsteps and continue to build the greatest middle class in world history?

No Child Left Behind

The effectiveness of our educational system is the single most important factor in determining whether our country will have a prosperous future. I say this statement without any reservations. After World War II, our previous generations believed this fact to be self-evident which is why they pursued coordinated governmental programs which would make higher education accessible to all Americans. They also sought to improve the education on all level for every citizen, by giving minorities, women and income-disadvantaged individuals equal opportunities at a better education through the investment of tax dollars in the upgrade and rehabilitation of facilities and curriculum. However, over the last 30 years, the United States has lessened its emphasis on educating the entire population and has followed policies of slashing educational funding or leaving it up to states to structure the educational curriculum for their citizens. These policies have left the U.S. ranked near the bottom on the list of industrialized countries in educational proficiency in both mathematics and science.

President Bush did recognize this failing in our system and tried through his legislative program called "No Child Left Behind" to provide a remedy to our struggling educational system. His fellow Republicans in Congress voted for the program, but failed to provide enough funding to properly institute all the tough provisions of the law. This oversight left the states and municipalities without the resources to handle the consequences of not adhering to the high test standards of the provision. In addition, the law required proficiency testing every year from the 4th grade to the 8th grade, tying federal school funding to the results of the testing. This requirement placed unwarranted emphasis on making all school curriculums strictly structured to passing the test. While requiring magnet and charter schools which were also receiving federal funding to follow the same guidelines, the government did not provide enough resources to quickly close those magnet and charter schools which failed to meet the requirements. This lack of consequence gave the magnet and charter schools a distinct advantage over the public schools in a given area. For these and many other reasons, the program, though well-intentioned, did not have the desired results and left many fiscal burdens on local governments.

Although President Obama did not agree with many of the areas of emphasis in the "No Child Left Behind" legislation, he and Congress have moved very slowly to remove and replace the bill. He has, however, through the Department of Education given states the latitude to waive the most burdensome portions of the legislation. In addition, through his "Race to the Top" program President Obama has tried to create Universal Preschool in an attempt to close the achievement gap. In order to build a new program, President Obama wants to have more input from local municipalities and teachers, who are on the frontline of the educational battle. But the President has not found the opportunity to bring these groups together and develop a new program.

Much of President Obama's emphasis in his first term has been on making higher education more accessible to every American. He has eliminated the private sector participation in the student loan program, which has freed up millions of dollars for Pell grants and other government grant programs. Also, by passing the "American Opportunity Tax Credit," a refundable tax credit for the first $4000 of a college education, he has given every American regardless of income access to higher education. Hence, these programs have enabled many disadvantaged and low-income students to get post-secondary education.

On the campaign trail, President Obama and Governor Romney have very different views of the educational system. Both do want to repeal "No Child Left Behind", but President

Obama as a senator voted against the major proposal of the Romney educational plan, which is "School choice." School choice is where parents can take a voucher and use the proceeds to send their children to private schools. This voucher program, like all voucher programs which the Republicans champion, would basically kill the public school system which previous generations fought so desperately to build. Those parents who have the means to use this program would withdraw their funding from the public school system, leaving only those who could not afford to leave the public schools and those who try to keep the public system alive. But eventually even those who want to support the system would have to leave due to the lack of resources in the system, or our indebted government would have to add more resources to replace the dollars which went to private schools. Either way the system would be destroyed due to the limitation of resources and our present achievement gaps would become larger and larger, creating a society of haves and have nots. Begging the question is America not about everyone aspiring to become a have?

World View

Obama Gets Osama

On May 1, 2003 President George W Bush proclaimed "Mission Accomplished" from the flight deck of USS Abraham Lincoln after its return from the Persian Gulf. President Bush prematurely declared the end of combat operations in Iraq. On this day, most Americans, including myself, were confused about what mission he was actually pronouncing accomplished, because for most of us the mission which President Bush was supposed to be carrying out was to bring to justice those who openly admitted to brutally murdering 3000 Americans on September 11. Instead, the Bush administration, at the end of their term, left the American people saddled with two wars which we could not afford or wanted and still no justice for our victims and their families. After seven years following the 9/11 attacks, the leaders of the terrorist organization, Al Qaida, which masterminded the attacks, were still at large and were repeatedly and defiantly broadcasting messages about their hatred of America, basically, mocking our inability to take revenge for our fallen. Therefore, essentially, the Bush administration had not accomplished anything which they had told the American people were their objectives.

President Obama and his administration were faced with trying to end two ongoing wars, while still dealing with a dangerous terrorist organization, which, although pushed into hiding in Afghanistan, was metastasizing in other countries around the globe. Ironically, Al Qaida, which had not been in Iraq prior to our ill-conceived invasion, was now one of the major forces that we were facing in Iraq. The Bush administration created the situation they proclaimed was in Iraq in the first place. The military leaders at the end of the Bush administration devised a military strategy to dramatically increase the number of troops in the combat zone in order to overpower the enemy combatants. Fortunately, with this strategy and with the cooperation of different factions in Iraq, we were able to gain control of the country and restore a functional central government. However, unlike Afghanistan, Iraq had a functional central government prior to our war, even though we did not agree with its politics, so the Iraqis wanted a central government in order to restore some form of normalcy to their lives. Thus, under the watch of the Obama administration, the Iraq war was ended as promised by candidate Obama during his election campaign.

In contrast, the Afghanis have never in 6000 years or so had a stable central government; all they know is the chaos of war and upheaval, and constantly, being conquered by one group or another. This is their sense of normalcy. As a result, for us to believe that we have the ability to install a stable central government is absolutely arrogant and an overreach of our interest. I truly do not believe that President Obama has this belief which is why he has established 2014 as our deadline for troop withdrawals, regardless of the condition of the central government. As a student of history, President Obama knows that a government is just a reflection of its people and unless the Afghanis themselves impose their will and demand a government, no outside force can create one.

Our infusion of ourselves in this region has had destabilizing effects throughout other countries in the area. Specifically, we have affected Pakistan and Iran by making both countries defensive with respect to our possible influence in the area. In Pakistan, the government over the years walked a fine line between their relationship with the U.S. and their relationship with the factions in the region. Thus, when we put them in a position of having to choose between helping us capture the groups which we had declared our enemies and helping those same groups which had cooperated with the Pakistani government to manage the outskirts of their territory, the Pakistanis chose to play both sides. The Americans were going to go home one day and leave these groups and the Pakistani government still having to interact with each other.

Similarly, Iran is likewise uncomfortable with our presence in the region. With Iraq no longer the power in the region, there becomes a power void, which Iran wants to fill. However, the U.S. wants to choose who will fill this power void and it definitely will not be Iran, so this is why the US and Iran are at odds. We must have an influence in the end which country fills the power void in the region. But Iran in the meanwhile constantly tries to increase its muscle might and recognition in the area.

With all this turmoil and drama transpiring in the region, President Obama never lost sight of the original purpose of this mission, which was to retaliate for all Americans and receive some closure for the victims and their families of 9/11. Consequently, on May 2, 2011, President Obama gave the order to our Special Services to decapitate Al Qaida. At about 1 am local time, Special Forces killed Osama Bin Ladin, the most wanted man in the world. Without much pomp and circumstance, President Obama accomplished the mission that President Bush could not.

"Mission Accomplished, President Obama"

Keep our Friends Close and ….

The technological advancements of the last 50 years have given rise to the most integrated global economy in the history of human civilization. Movement of capital and products throughout the world has reached an all-time high in both amount and velocity. The resulting level of interdependency between countries has made us truly a world comprised of nation-states participating in a single world economy. The effects of economic tremors in one country can be felt as aftershocks in another. Therefore, it is now imperative to engage and cooperate with each participant in the global marketplace. Thus, each player in the economic arena must be ready to negotiate mutually beneficial arrangements which will enable their countries to reap the value of these trade partnerships for generations to come. It is, hence, necessary for countries to take a long-term view with regard to receiving the full rewards of any relationship.

Developing strong trade alliances with friends and foes alike is vital in order for America to maintain its stature as the leading economic power in the world. As a result, the US must be conscious of labeling any country ally or enemy. We must always assess the economic repercussions of any such designations. Being mindful of our position in the world will and has been the means by which we can sustain our economic advantage. Governor Romney on the campaign trail is spewing very tough rhetoric with respect to the second largest economy in the world, namely China. Not to mention that they are the largest nondomestic holder of our national debt. Mr. Romney is advocating that in a Romney administration there would be tariffs placed on cheap Chinese goods, and he would also institute tough sanctions on China in order to stop their currency manipulation. Specifically, Governor Romney wants to stop China from pegging their currency to the US dollar, which is done to ensure that their currency will never reach a higher value than ours. Consequently, this low currency value places an artificial price deflator on their goods and services, enabling their products to maintain a lower price with respect to US products.

Although this behavior is obvious market manipulation merely with the intention of enabling China to foster a high single digit or low double digit growth rate, our short-term loses will be offset by our long-term gains which we receive from the ongoing relationship. President Obama, as did many presidents before him, recognizes that this policy approach is in the national interest of the United States. He realizes that only through dialogue, negotiations and open complaints to the World Trade

Organization and not through an unwarranted trade war would the interest of the nation be best advanced. President Obama through numerous visits to China by Secretary Clinton has been able to keep the Chinese markets open to U.S. businesses. For example, General Motors, who entered the Chinese car market in 2004, sold over 2 million cars in 2010 and anticipates more than doubling that amount to over 5 million units by 2015. Thousands and thousands of other American businesses are working to enter the Chinese markets in order to reap the future benefits.

Furthermore, as a result of this high growth rate, China will continue to grow their enormous middle class, and as this middle class enlarges in both quantity and purchasing power the demand of this group for goods and services will provide US businesses incredible opportunities to expand their market share. In addition, the demands from this middle class will inevitable shrink the trade deficit between the two countries; just as the trade deficits were reduced between the U.S. and European countries after those countries recovered from World War II. So Mr. Romney's short-run actions would only result in unnecessary retaliations between the two partners, causing unfortunate consequences for the citizens of both nations.

Governor Romney's inability to show even the most basic understanding of foreign economic policy is also demonstrated in his comments about how the U.S. will be in the same debt crisis as countries in European Union, if Obama wins. First of all, the crisis in the EU is basically a result of them now having a single currency, coupled with the inability of individual EU members to collect enough tax dollars to pay for all the services which their governments are providing; so with respect to this latter cause, Mr. Romney's tax-cut promises are more detrimental to this nation's debt situation than President Obama's fiscal policies.

Simply, the EU debt crisis is the result of having a single currency, the euro. If Greece, or the other countries suffering from debt problems, had their own currency, they would be experiencing an immediate and drastic devaluation in the currency. This reduction would cause inflation in their countries, but they would not be able to export these price hikes to other countries. They would also be able to satisfy current account deficits by paying in their currency; thus, isolating their financial problems within their borders. However, since they have to pay all debts in euros they have to generate enough euros through transaction exchange; as a result their inflation can be exported to all the other countries in the EU. This inflation possibility and currency devaluation causes individual debt problems to become an *EU debt crisis* because price hikes could be permeated all over the EU; thus, resulting in a possible default on the debts by many member countries.

In contrast, the U.S. pays all debts in dollars, a marketable means of exchange, so debt repayment is always possible. Furthermore, we manage our own monetary production through our central bank, allowing for a uniformed controlled monetary policy. The EU's monetary production is dominated by Germany which has a historic aversion to hyperinflation. Consequently, Germany assumes the role of our central bank and controls the EU monetary policy. The individual countries maintain independent fiscal policies which results in uncoordinated economic policy. Hence, in order to maintain currency value and control inflation, Germany will have to bailout the other member nation-states. If Governor Romney wanted to be more accurate concerning the situation, a better analogy would be California is our Greece.

Nobel Laureate

President Obama's election meant more than the election of another American president; it signified the dawning of an era where anyone who has the will and desire could achieve the most powerful office in the world. The election did not mean the end of discrimination; however, it did represent the end of the "glass ceiling." This new feeling of hope was not only perceived here in the United States, but also felt throughout the world. This recognition of *"anything is possible"* was echoed by the Nobel Committee when they gave President Obama the Nobel Peace Prize so early in his presidency. They admittedly gave President Obama this acknowledgment prematurely due to the great promise which his presidency represented to all the nations of the world. By awarding President Obama in anticipation of the significance of his presidency, the Nobel Committee set the foundation for the incredible changes which have taken place under his watch.

Although many would argue that it is just a coincidence, the *"Arab Spring"* of freedom represents one of those incredible transformations, which President Obama cannot openly take credit for the uprisings; however, the sense of hope that his presidency gave to the world in some way may have inspired a few of those who marched in the streets against the tyranny and oppression of their governments. These oppositional groups refused to bow to the forces of the dictatorships which ruled their countries with unrelenting cruelty. They stood strong as they were beaten and bombed by the forces loyal to their leaders. This *Arab Spring* obviously draws parallels to the civil rights movement of the 1960s. The oppressed masses fought unwaveringly to overcome the decades of inequality and hopelessness in order to have a better future for their children. As in the civil rights movement, the victory of freedom could only be achieved through the perseverance of those who would no longer accept their oppression.

President Obama to the dismay of many established leaders in the Middle East stood strong behind those who were oppressed giving them the backbone and support necessary to help their voices be heard. This support came at a price because many of the leaders which were removed from power, for example in Egypt, were long-time allies of the United States, and the resulting democracies represented an uncertain future. But the voices of the people could not be silenced and our values of individual freedom could not be ignored.

President Obama acted when he had to as in Libya and stayed on the outside when the situation required minimal interference as in Egypt. Even now in Syria with the battles waging between the opposing armies, the Obama administration is leading the world in condemning the mass death and destruction of the governmental forces; however, President Obama is careful not to put the United States in the middle of another country's civil war. Any action of force on either side would compromise the interest of the United States and not be beneficial to our ultimate goals in the region. America is much better served by being identified as a promoter of freedom and not as a killer of the Muslim people. Many groups in the Middle East would want to draw America into this conflict just to change the focus from the true issues in this war. President Obama knows that America cannot be baited into making such a tactical mistake. Some political opponents of President Obama have indicated that they believe the United States should act more aggressively than we have, but such opinions are very misguided and do not have the welfare of the United States as their primary consideration.

Even now as we mourn the death of our fallen ambassador and our other citizens in Libya, we must not act hastily or too broadly to avenge their death. We must identify those who murdered our citizens and bring them to justice without condemning all the people who would be our allies. The *Arab Spring* should exhibit, if nothing else, to us and the rest of the world that most of the people of the Middle East relish the same values of freedom as we covet so greatly.

In order for America to maintain its safety and insure its role as a symbol for freedom, we must continue to have a leader who recognizes when to act, but also knows when actions are not warranted because the price of those actions is too grave. President Obama has demonstrated such a resolve. The Republican presidential candidate advocates returning to our hawkish stance which was the *"Bush Doctrine."* Namely, America should attack first and ask questions later. This policy got us into two unwinnable wars, killed over 6,000 American soldiers and seriously injured over 30,000 more. Is returning to this philosophy worth the price?

The Other Guys

Here We Go Again

Have we not seen this play before? Are we not just living through the same acts over again? The Republicans again are trying to tarnish a sitting incumbent Democratic president by using taxpayers' money and an overinflated sense of authority to bring us on another one of their witch hunts. Did we not have to live through this just over a decade ago when a Republican-controlled House of Representative went after a president in order to do nothing more than reduces his political appeal? At that time it was justified by showing their outrage for his behavior through having a Congressional theatrical performance of a fabricated impeachment trial. This time their Congressional performance appears to be in the form of a voodoo ritual. Since they cannot find any issue to directly connect President Obama to, they will go after a surrogate, calling the performance "Contempt of Congress."

After rigorous searching, the Republican majority in the House of Representatives has been unable to find a single damning issue that they could tie directly to President Obama. So with time running out they had to create their own voodoo doll of the President, and unfortunately Attorney General Holder is the person that looks the most like the president in the administration. As in all voodoo rituals, the Republicans will try to stick pins in their voodoo doll and hope that each pin prick in Attorney General Holder will be able to induce some sort of political injury to President Obama, or at least maim his re-election chances in some way.

Although this performance is unique in its approach, it is not unique in its goal. We just need to think back a short 14 or so years ago when the Republican-controlled House of Representatives in a very similar situation of facing an incumbent Democratic president, dragged the rest of the nation through the unnecessary impeachment hearings of President Clinton for crimes that did not in any way reach the constitutional standard of "High Crimes and Misdemeanors." As history has demonstrated, this stunt was just a political play to weaken a strong incumbent Democratic president, and unfortunately, they were rewarded for their deceptive actions, which only fed into the Republican "win-at-all-cost" mentality. As a result, they have since become emboldened and will use their power to obstruct progress or as a means to grab more power.

Representative Issa is now playing the dual roles of voodoo doctor and the modern-day Ken Starr. As we all watch his performance and the acts of the play unfold, we all know how it is going to end. The Republican leadership will find Attorney General Holder in "Contempt of Congress," and then they will pursue Attorney General Holder to the full extent of the powers allowed to Congress, even threatening to imprison the Attorney General in the jail in the basement of the Capitol, all the while, reiterating in news conference after news conference that if the administration would just choose to cooperate with our unreasonable requests, this fact-finding witch hunt could all end. Every day they will be gaining more and more airtime, print space and news coverage. In the end, the whole ordeal would be for nothing except to convince their Republican base that President Obama is not only non-American and unpatriotic but now a criminal. Many will want to believe this because he could be nothing else, being black, of course, he must be a criminal. This they hope will energize those true Americans to work harder and get to the polls to remove this undeserving, shameful president from office. Additionally, in a perfect world this performance could persuade those right-leaning independent voters who were on the fence that they must come out and vote against this non-

American, unpatriotic, criminal president, and stop him from further defacing the Office of President.

We have definitely seen this play before. It is just a different spin on the same theme, instead of going directly after the main character; this plot is based on attacking the main character through a similar-looking minor character, their form of a voodoo ritual. But the goal for both of these performances are the same, namely to politically injure the incumbent Democratic president. How long are we going to just be an audience and allow these deceitful and conniving abuses of power to continue? We must ask ourselves, are these uses of congressional power in the best interest of our country? These witch hunts must energize everyone who considers themselves a progressive American, because as we have seen there is no action outside the bounds of their political game. Anything that will gain them further power is in play, because in their minds the end justifies the means.

Why Bain Matters

There has been much written and spoken about Governor Romney's years at Bain Capital. Most of the debate, initiated by Mr. Romney himself, attempts to prove that, due to his time starting, running and owning Bain Capital, he has the best experience to address the economic issues which face our country. I think I, like many Americans, have basically started to tune out most of the coverage of the Bain debate because the focus of the news programs is not what makes Bain a relevant topic of discussion. Governor Romney wants us to believe that just because he was in the private sector running a company, he is qualified to run the country, as if the President of the United States of America is just another CEO position. The news reporters allow him to take for granted this assumption. In addition, Mr. Romney has the audacity to argue that after spearheading the growth of his company and hiring all the executives and managers he has no responsibility for their subsequent actions only a short time after relinquishing daily operational control, even though he still owned the company.

The debate over Bain is not whether this experience gave Governor Romney an understanding of the economy, because, obviously, the view of economic issues from one corporate window is completely different from the view of the economy from the seat above the corporate jungle. The president of the United States must take into consideration the welfare of all corporations and consumers, not just consider the needs of a single entity. As a side note, many would have us believe that the decisions of a single corporation are always in the best interest of the country, but this notion is completely false. A corporation's singular purpose is to maximize shareholder value through the maximization of profits. If in the off chance that this single purpose coincides with the interest of the nation as a whole, that is great; however, the interest of the nation is only taken into account with respect to its impact on shareholder value. Consequently, to say this experience qualifies someone to guide the economy of the nation is simply ridiculous.

The relevance of Bain is in the culture, attitude and people that Governor Romney fostered at Bain Capital. These are the substantive experiences that translate to being president of the United States. The president is not only the head executive of the nation he is the symbolic leader of the country and the world. He must lead by both example and deeds. The first and foremost decision a president makes is what kind of administration he wants the American people to remember years after his presidency is over. This decision establishes the culture and attitude of his presidency. For example, President George W. Bush was very uncomfortable addressing the media and speaking impromptu, so he avoided interaction with the media and as a result, had very few news conferences through which to keep Americans informed. Thus, everyone in his administration seemed to do the same. In contrast, President Obama enjoys addressing the media and also enjoys improvisation, which is evident in the more open nature of his administration. This culture and attitude is then further illustrated and enhanced by the people the president appoints to the various positions in the executive branch. These appointees, along with the culture and attitude of the presidency, are reflected not only during his administration but act as his legacy for historians to debate far into the future.

If we examine Bain Capital as Romney's example of how he would establish and organize his administration, we would have to be very concerned that the Romney administration would be the most closed and secretive administration in the history of the United States. Furthermore, the attitude of the administration would be an emphasis on the short-term goals of the few not the long-term welfare of the nation. This conclusion is completely evident if one just quickly examines the operations of Bain. Romney started and built Bain Capital to use their access to capital as immediately as possible to invest in struggling companies which had hidden value in order to quickly reap a sizable return on their investment. Bain was never expecting to be a long-term investor in any of the acquisitions; only after they reaped their initial return and the company still had inherent value would they invest for the long-run. But the long run survival of the company being acquired was not relevant to Bain's profit decision. Romney would be the face of the acquisition but his other executives would covertly act as the corporate raiders, sending the company into bankruptcy, if needed, in order to free the assets of any burdens which may be attached to them. When the assets were free of previous encumbrances, Bain would then take their initial investment and a considerable return before anyone else was paid, so that they could ensure their return on investment; in the end, leaving the company with a massive debt situation to overcome.

Is this truly the kind of experience that we want in the White House? Romney's Bain experience if transformed into the presidency would be President Romney telling us how he is going to save Medicare while Vice President Ryan takes all the money out of the program to give to his rich investors or donors. Oh right, that is exactly what he is planning to do once elected as stated in the Ryan budget. Specifically, Romney is going to initiate massive cuts to programs, like Medicare, where it becomes a voucher program and Medicare recipients must find private insurers, while giving his rich donors a return on their investment, additional massive tax breaks for the wealthy. Like so many of his previous acquisitions, can America survive the Romney takeover, with Romney taking back his initial investment and a large profit from the U.S. Treasury?

Let Them Fail

> *If General Motors, Ford and Chrysler get the bailout that*
> *their chief executives asked for yesterday, you can kiss*
> *the American automotive industry goodbye. It won't go*
> *overnight, but its demise will be virtually guaranteed.*

> \-   *Mitt Romney*

Is this the man to whom we should entrust the leadership of the entire U.S. economy? I will give Mr. Romney the benefit of the doubt that when he wrote this opinion he was not attempting to say we should just let the American automotive industry simply dissolve; he was actually trying to point out that government should have no role in the operation of private corporations, and we should merely let the mechanisms already in the system deal with the problems of the companies. Although I do disagree with this contention also, at least he is not emphatically condemning all the employees and the numerous other companies which depend on this industry to perish in the aftermath of their destruction. But Mr. Romney's statement of certain demise is without precedent because he should remember that it was President Reagan who gave the bailout loan to Chrysler in the early '80s, which saved the company for the next 30 years. Furthermore, I believe Mr. Romney is naïve to think the executives of these corporations wanted to invite the government into their board rooms. These chief executives must have tried every other avenue available before they came to the conclusion that the only alternative to a total collapse was to ask the government for aid. As we all know government aid comes with many strings attached.

Governor Romney's article, if my interpretation is correct, does beg the bigger question of whether government does have a role in the bailout of corporations and banks which are deemed too intertwined in our society to be allowed to fail? Clearly, we can see from the article that Mr. Romney believes such failures of major corporations or banks should just be permitted to happen under the normal operations of the market system, and the bankruptcy process should be allowed to proceed. But is not the entire bankruptcy structure a government imposition into the operations of the markets? Simply, bankruptcy is where the government steps in as an intermediary between private market participants in order to adjudicate the allocation of assets and liabilities of a failing corporation or individual. So certainly there must be a role for government in these processes. Then, Mr. Romney essentially is only saying that government should not lend taxpayers dollars to corporations that require assistance which cannot be helped through any other means. However, the government provides this assistance all the time to corporations through the Small Business Administration, FEMA in times of natural disasters and the Federal Reserve does this type of lending for banks through the discount window in order to maintain liquidity in the system.

Obviously, Mr. Romney's view of the role of government in the operations of a market economy is not consistent with the reality of our present system. The government plays a vital role in the proper operations of the markets. The almost disastrous consequences of our deregulated Wall Street derivative markets are evidence of that fact. The government plays many roles in a market economy, and in the case of these extraordinary circumstances the government had to play the role of *"lender of last resort."* These roles of government are necessary because government's most important and basically only purpose is to guarantee the betterment of the society as a whole, which sometimes means that it must step into the markets in order to insure the interest of the whole society is correctly secured.

From this article it is apparent that Mr. Romney does not understand the simple concept that what is in the interest of individual parts of the economy may not be in the interest of the whole economy. He has only had the experience of looking at the world from inside one corporate window and has not been able to bring himself above the buildings to see the entire landscape. If he had he would realize the importance of government in our economy, and not purely try to downplay the positive effects government has in the proper operations of the markets.

Hence, I ask the question again: do we truly want to put Mr. Romney in charge of the operations of our entire economy? He already wants to relinquish all the responsibilities of the job. Governor Romney is applying for a job for which he wants to eliminate many of the duties, so why is he spending so much to get the job of president only to try to lessen its importance? He must be trying to save us from ourselves.

Drill, Baby, Drill

Oil price are again soaring out of control staying well above $90 per barrel. As a result, pump prices are threatening to stay higher than $4 per gallon putting an unstated tax on the American economy. These high fuel costs are being felt adversely throughout the economy. The transportation of goods to market is becoming more and more costly, causing an increase in the price levels of all the goods and services we use every day. These continued high pump prices will further slow the growth of a weak economy. Also, these high prices have renewed the calls for more domestic oil production in order to gain energy independence from Middle Eastern oil producers. However, the good news surrounding these high gasoline prices is that we have never produced so much domestic oil. Our production of domestic oil is at an all-time high and growing.

President Obama can boast that under his administration, we are importing approximately 1 million fewer barrels of oil each day, and producing more oil domestically which by 2020 will grow to 6.7 million barrels a day. Although I would love to give President Obama sole credit for this weaning off of foreign oil, the truth is we are obviously using less oil in this slow economy and more importantly, at these high prices domestic oil production becomes profitable for oil companies. The global oil market truly dictates where oil comes from around the world. The Middle Eastern oil producers can extract and refine oil at a cheaper price than we can due to their reduced labor and environmental cost, so when international oil prices are low it is advantageous for oil companies to buy oil from the global market place rather than produce it domestically. Conversely, during soaring oil prices like now, oil companies make more profits by exploring domestic oil options.

Republicans want us to believe that if we merely open our lands and waters to domestic oil production this will cause oil prices to miraculously drop and we will become energy independent. This is simply not the case. The oil market is actually a global market and only at these high global prices is it cost effective for domestic oil producers to compete in the marketplace. At lower prices oil companies will just buy their oil on the global market and save their domestic oil production for when oil prices increase. There is more profit in buying this foreign oil and importing it into the US than trying to produce the oil domestically. Additionally, the oil companies will not permit an oversupply of oil in the market either. They require high oil price, specifically a continually escalating price scale, in order to continue and exceed profit gains of the previous year. To eliminate excess supply, oil companies shut down production either globally or domestically, they lessen refining capacity or they plainly buy less oil to bring to the pumps.

Many would say that my assessment of the oil market has a hint of conspiracy theory, but the truth is that the global oil markets are dominated by only a few mega-sized multinational companies. These companies are structured such that each company has a production, refining and retail division and each division assesses their profitability independent of the other divisions. So basically, the refining division buys the cheapest oil available to sell to the retail division and in turn the retail division tries to purchase the cheapest refined oil to make the most profits possible. Thus, if the production division cannot produce the oil at a competitive price for the refining division, the oil company will merely halt production until prices warrant additional operations. There is nothing wrong with this for the oil company, because for the company this is maximizing profits, which is their sole objective. However, consequently, our oil independence is only likely if oil prices continue to rise higher and higher.

True independence will only be possible with complete energy independence. Meaning, what we need is to be weaned off of oil entirely. Drilling any more will never solve our oil addiction; we have to, as President Obama outlines in his energy program, find new renewable forms of energy. The old forms of energy are just perpetuating our addictive personalities. We must embrace wind, hydrogen, light and nuclear, and in the short-run use natural gas or coal as we cure ourselves from the side effects of our recovery. Only through a complete and coordinated treatment program to eventually move the entire country away from oil usage will we be able to be free ourselves from the influences of our dealers, the oil companies.

Bush Policies on Steroids

On the last night of the Republican National Convention, I watched with anticipation as Governor Romney, now crowned Presidential Nominee Romney, delivered his greatly awaited acceptance speech. I had the hope that he would enlighten us with his policy objectives and provide the specifics of how he was going to change the current course of our nation. But as I listened to his speech all I heard was "elect me I will be better than the other guy," and when he was not saying that, when he actually said things which outlined specific policy objectives all I could imagine was George W. Bush outlining the same tired policies in State of the Union speeches over and over again. "Cut taxes, cut taxes, cut taxes" and cut government spending, it is the path to solving all of our problems. How does this solve our education gap, how does this solve our crumbling infrastructure, how does this solve our bankrupt entitlement programs, how does this solve any of the problems facing our nation. Tell me, I want to know! Plainly, we are still under the Bush tax policies where the tax code is completely focused on giving incentives to investors and business owners to invest and do business, something they would do anyway because they are investors and business owners.

President Obama has not been able to change any of these Bush tax policies; all he has been able to do is add some stimuli to the Bush economy which is the only reason he was able to stop the plummeting Bush employment numbers. President Bush could not create a single job with his economic policies, and Nominee Romney now wants to continue the Bush policies with even more tax cuts, no stimulus and deep cuts to government spending. Did we not already have eight years of this? It was Einstein who said, "The true sign of insanity is doing the same thing over again and expecting a different result." Are we completely insane?

Many would argue that we cannot blame our economic problems on President Bush, but to them I would shout, *"Yes we can."* His legacy has been the framework under which we have had to live. President Clinton did not leave him with this mess. There was a government surplus, a growing economy and a path to solving our future problems. Their reply would be well there was 9/11, and I agree. However, if President Bush just focused on bringing those to justice who caused 9/11 and not fighting unnecessary wars and not giving unnecessary tax cuts, in the first place, we would have the resources to handle our future problems. Nominee Romney now wants to give even further tax cuts which will leave us more vulnerable to the unexpected future events. Suppose we have to overcome a situation which is worse than 9/11: are we going to have the resources to handle those potential catastrophic occurrences?

The Romney agenda has no basis in reality. He says again and again, "government does not create jobs," but the companies which pave the roads who depend on a government contracts sure do create jobs. The business owner who needs that road in order for his business to be accessible sure does create jobs. Government spending is a vital part of the economy. The private sector alone cannot handle all that is necessary to keep the country growing. Certain things like road construction which are in the public good are not profitable enough, unless we put tolls on every road, for the private sector to undertake, so this is a necessary function of government. Obviously, government creates jobs because these and many others are functions of government which must be done by someone so a job or many jobs must be created in order to accomplish the necessary role of government. Whether this is done as efficiently as possible is another job for someone else to do who is in a position to oversee this function.

Once and for all, can we please say with a single voice that the conservative economic policy agenda does not work? All it does is create a backwards income-redistribution model. It takes from the poor and the middle class and gives to the rich. This income model will turn any country into a corrupt third world country in just a few generations. These policies create a country with a rich elite upper class and everyone else fighting for the scraps which *"trickle down"* from their overindulgent tables. Is this the America our founders envisioned? Is this the America so many generations have given their lives for? Is this the America that beckoned immigrants to its shores, who wanted an opportunity to achieve the DREAM which is only found in America?

Embrace Our Moment

The gauntlet has been slammed down, the die has been cast; the choice in the election of 2012 is now crystal clear. We must embrace our moment and plot a course away from these failed conservative ideas. Governor Romney has now decisively drawn a line in the sand with his choice of Representative Paul Ryan as his running mate. If there was a question about his intentions and positions before, this Vice Presidential candidate without a doubt plainly defines his agenda. This choice is a symbolic bullhorn to all those who do not want a return of the years of W to get organized and motivated immediately. The Romney-Ryan ticket, through their endorsement of the Ryan Budget Plan, is now transparently illuminating their intention to dismantle the social safety net programs of the last 50 years and finish the transference of burden from the wealthy to the middle class that was started under Reagan and continued under W.

The Ryan budget would reward those who need no further reward. It would give the wealthiest Americans unnecessary additional marginal rate tax cuts and capital gain rate cuts, while taking away from those, who can least afford it, programs that are essential to their existence, such as Medicare and Medicaid. The budget blames all of our debt problems on the spending side of the ledger without taking into account that the federal government is collecting the least amount of revenues as a percentage of Gross Domestic Product in the last 50 years. If the Reagan years and the Bush "43" years were any indication, the debt which would result from these additional tax cuts will only grow our debt crisis exponentially into a complete apocalypse.

The Ryan budget also would place further burdens on the budgets of states and municipalities, which are already strapped from the Bush tax cuts. States and municipalities would have to lay off teachers, policemen, firefighters, and other government workers in order to try to balance their budgets. The resulting cascade effect would decimate local economies, already hard hit. Furthermore, these layoffs would not be enough, so the local governments would have to raise taxes, such as property taxes and sales taxes, thusly impacting the vast majority of their citizens, middle class households. Consequently, in the end, these additional tax cuts would result in tax increases on the middle class, making the cost of living for the middle class rise even higher. Simply, just as the Bush tax cuts had done during the last decade, and the Reagan tax cuts during the 1980s, the middle class invariably will shoulder the burden for these unnecessary tax cuts to the wealthy.

To make matters worse, the Ryan Budget Plan makes unsubstantiated and unprovable claims about employment increases. But if history is any guide, as after the Bush tax cuts, this plan will create no new jobs because there will be very little demand in the economy. The middle class will not spend their income except on absolutely necessary goods and services because they will be overburdened by the tax increases they will have to bear from the local communities and their other cost of living increases. Additionally, as in the Bush years, incomes of middle-class workers will be stagnant, and the lingering unemployment will cause them to constantly live in fear of losing their jobs. As a result, they will be unable to demand cost-of-living wage increases. Government sector demand will be nonexistent because of the extreme nature of these spending cuts. The Republicans may try to maintain some government demand as Reagan and Bush administrations tried through military spending. However, this spending will have much less effect as during the Bush years due to the fact that the military sector remains a much smaller proportion of the overall economy as compared to before the 1990s, when the military sector was reduced by the Clinton administration.

History illustrates over and over again that the policy direction which is being proposed by the Romney-Ryan ticket is doomed to failure. Many proponents of tax cuts want to focus on the growth of the economy after marginal tax rates were cut by Kennedy administration in the previous century, but they fail to take into account the massive growth that was occurring because of the demand by the new middle class for services in both the private and public sectors. This growing middle class drove demand in the economy. Additionally during the Reagan years, the military sector was a higher proportion of our economy, so building up the military as President Reagan did, stimulated demand throughout the greater economy. This is simply not the case anymore. Tax cuts alone or even coupled with military spending increases, without growth in the consumer sectors, which is now the overwhelmingly largest proportion of the economy or other government spending directed at consumers, will have limited efficacy, leaving the economy vulnerable to dramatic swings in the business cycle.

Embrace our moment. These policies are not new or bold. They are the same conservative agenda of the last 30 years reprinted under a new cover. It is our responsibility as it was the responsibility of the Americans of the Civil War to fight for the welfare and future of our nation. Those citizens on the surface fought to end slavery, but equally important fought to stop the expansion of the conservative agricultural economy of the South and to promote the growth of the new dynamic industrial economy of the North; as a result, opening the door to the incredible industrial revolution of the 20th century. It is our moment now to open the door to our dynamic economic future, and stop the further development of the failed conservative economy of the past. We must get energized in order to prevail in our "Modern Civil War."